Francis Frith's
CARMARTHENSHIRE

PHOTOGRAPHIC MEMORIES

Francis Frith's
CARMARTHENSHIRE

◆

John A Milnes

FRITH
BOOK Co

First published in the United Kingdom in 2000 by
Frith Book Company Ltd

Hardback Edition 2000
ISBN 1-85937-216-3

Paperback Edition 2002
ISBN 1-85937-604-5

Reprinted in hardback 2002

British Library Cataloguing in Publication Data

Francis Frith's Carmarthenshire
John A Milnes

Frith Book Company Ltd
Frith's Barn, Teffont,
Salisbury, Wiltshire SP3 5QP
Tel: +44 (0) 1722 716 376
Email: info@francisfrith.co.uk
www.francisfrith.co.uk

Printed and bound in Great Britain

Contents

Francis Frith: *Victorian Pioneer*

FRANCIS FRITH, Victorian founder of the world-famous photographic archive, was a complex and mult-talented man. A devout Quaker and a highly successful Victorian businessman, he was both philosophic by nature and pioneering in outlook.

By 1855 Francis Frith had already established a wholesale grocery business in Liverpool, and sold it for the astonishing sum of £200,000, which is the equivalent today of over £15,000,000. Now a multi-millionaire, he was able to indulge his passion for travel. As a child he had pored over travel books written by early explorers, and his fancy and imagination had been stirred by family holidays to the sublime mountain regions of Wales and Scotland. 'What a land of spirit-stirring and enriching scenes and places!' he had written. He was to return to these scenes of grandeur in later years to 'recapture the thousands of vivid and tender memories', but with a different purpose. Now in his thirties, and captivated by the new science of photography, Frith set out on a series of pioneering journeys to the Nile regions that occupied him from 1856 until 1860.

Intrigue and Adventure

He took with him on his travels a specially-designed wicker carriage that acted as both dark-room and sleeping chamber. These far-flung journeys were packed with intrigue and adventure. In his life story, written when he was sixty-three, Frith tells of being held captive by bandits, and of fighting 'an awful midnight battle to the very point of surrender with a deadly pack of hungry, wild dogs'. Sporting flowing Arab costume, Frith arrived at Akaba by camel seventy years before Lawrence, where he encountered 'desert princes and rival sheikhs, blazing with jewel-hilted swords'.

During these extraordinary adventures he was assiduously exploring the desert regions bordering the Nile and patiently recording the antiquities and peoples with his camera. He was the first photographer to venture beyond the sixth cataract. Africa was still the mysterious 'Dark Continent', and Stanley and Livingstone's historic meeting was a decade into the future. The conditions for picture taking confound belief. He laboured for hours in his wicker dark-room in the sweltering heat of the desert, while the volatile chemicals fizzed dangerously in their trays. Often he was forced to work in remote tombs and caves where conditions were cooler. Back in London he exhibited his photographs and was 'rapturously cheered' by members of the Royal Society. His reputation as a photographer was made overnight. An eminent modern historian has likened their impact on the population of the time to that on our own generation of the first photographs taken on the surface of the moon.

Venture of a Life-Time

Characteristically, Frith quickly spotted the opportunity to create a new business as a specialist publisher of photographs. He lived in an era of immense and sometimes violent change. For the poor in the early part of Victoria's reign work was a drudge and the hours long, and people had precious little free time to enjoy themselves. Most had no transport other than a cart or gig at their disposal, and had not travelled far beyond the boundaries of their own town or village.

However, by the 1870s, the railways had threaded their way across the country, and Bank Holidays and half-day Saturdays had been made obligatory by Act of Parliament. All of a sudden the ordinary working man and his family were able to enjoy days out and see a little more of the world.

With characteristic business acumen, Francis Frith foresaw that these new tourists would enjoy having souvenirs to commemorate their days out. In 1860 he married Mary Ann Rosling and set out with the intention of photographing every city, town and village in Britain. For the next thirty years he travelled the country by train and by pony and trap, producing fine photographs of seaside resorts and beauty spots that were keenly bought by millions of Victorians. These prints were painstakingly pasted into family albums and pored over during the dark nights of winter, rekindling precious memories of summer excursions.

The Rise of Frith & Co

Frith's studio was soon supplying retail shops all over the country. To meet the demand he gathered about him a small team of photographers, and published the work of independent artist-photographers of the calibre of Roger Fenton and Francis Bedford. In order to gain some understanding of the scale of Frith's business one only has to look at the catalogue issued by Frith & Co in 1886: it runs to some 670 pages, listing not only many thousands of views of the British Isles but also many photographs of most European countries, and China, Japan, the USA and Canada – note the sample page shown above

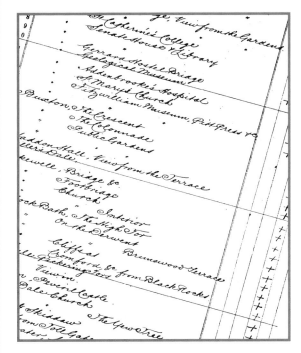

from the hand-written *Frith & Co* ledgers detailing pictures taken. By 1890 Frith had created the greatest specialist photographic publishing company in the world, with over 2,000 outlets – more than the combined number that Boots and W H Smith have today! The picture on the right shows the *Frith & Co* display board at Ingleton in the Yorkshire Dales. Beautifully constructed with mahogany frame and gilt inserts, it could display up to a dozen local scenes.

Postcard Bonanza

The ever-popular holiday postcard we know today took many years to develop. In 1870 the Post Office issued the first plain cards, with a pre-printed stamp on one face. In 1894 they allowed other publishers' cards to be sent through the mail with an attached adhesive halfpenny stamp. Demand grew rapidly, and in 1895 a new size of postcard was permitted

called the court card, but there was little room for illustration. In 1899, a year after Frith's death, a new card measuring 5.5 x 3.5 inches became the standard format, but it was not until 1902 that the divided back came into being, with address and message on one face and a full-size illustration on the other. *Frith & Co* were in the vanguard of postcard development, and Frith's sons Eustace and Cyril continued their father's monumental task, expanding the number of views offered to the public and recording more and more places in Britain, as the coasts and countryside were opened up to mass travel.

Francis Frith died in 1898 at his villa in Cannes, his great project still growing. The archive he created continued in business for another seventy years. By 1970 it contained over a third of a million pictures of 7,000 cities, towns and villages. The massive photographic record Frith has left to us stands as a living monument to a special and very remarkable man.

Frith's Archive: *A Unique Legacy*

FRANCIS FRITH'S legacy to us today is of immense significance and value, for the magnificent archive of evocative photographs he created provides a unique record of change in 7,000 cities, towns and villages throughout Britain over a century and more. Frith and his fellow studio photographers revisited locations many times down the years to update their views, compiling for us an enthralling and colourful pageant of British life and character.

We tend to think of Frith's sepia views of Britain as nostalgic, for most of us use them to conjure up memories of places in our own lives with which we have family associations. It often makes us forget that to Francis Frith they were records of daily life as it was actually being lived in the cities, towns and villages of his day. The Victorian age was one of great and often bewildering change for ordinary people, and

though the pictures evoke an impression of slower times, life was as busy and hectic as it is today.

We are fortunate that Frith was a photographer of the people, dedicated to recording the minutiae of everyday life. For it is this sheer wealth of visual data, the painstaking chronicle of changes in dress, transport, street layouts, buildings, housing, engineering and landscape that captivates us so much today. His remarkable images offer us a powerful link with the past and with the lives of our ancestors.

Today's Technology

Computers have now made it possible for Frith's many thousands of images to be accessed almost instantly. In the Frith archive today, each photograph is carefully 'digitised' then stored on a CD Rom. Frith archivists can locate a single photograph amongst thousands within seconds. Views can be catalogued and sorted under a variety of categories of place and content to the immediate benefit of researchers.

Inexpensive reference prints can be created for them at the touch of a mouse button, and a wide range of books and other printed materials assembled and published for a wider, more general readership - in the next twelve months over a hundred Frith local history titles will be published! The day-to-day workings of the archive are very different from how they were in Francis Frith's time: imagine the herculean task of sorting through eleven tons of glass negatives as Frith had to do to locate a

THE FRANCIS FRITH COLLECTION

Photographic publishers since 1860

HOME | PHOTO SEARCH | BOOKS | PORTFOLIO | GALLERY | MY CART
Products | History | Other Collections | Contact us | Help?

your town,
your village

365,000 photographs of 7,000 towns and villages, taken between 1860 & 1970.

The Frith Archive
The Frith Archive is the remarkable legacy of its energetic and visionary founder. Today, the Frith archive is the only nationally important archive of its kind still in private ownership.

The Collection is world-renowned for the extraordinary quality of its images.

The Gallery
This month The Frith Gallery features images from "Frith's Egypt".

the **FRITH**gallery

News...
Image update complete. An additional 5,000 images have been added and the quality of all images has now been improved.

Sample Chapters avaliable. The first selection of sample chapters from the Frith Book Co.'s extensive range is now available. All are offered in Pdf format for easy downloading and viewing.

explore FRITH
Search thousands of photographs from one of the worlds' great archives.

Town search
[   ] GO

County search
[Select a county ▼] GO

See Frith at www.francisfrith.co.uk

particular sequence of pictures! Yet the archive still prides itself on maintaining the same high standards of excellence laid down by Francis Frith, including the painstaking cataloguing and indexing of every view.

It is curious to reflect on how the internet now allows researchers in America and elsewhere greater instant access to the archive than Frith himself ever enjoyed. Many thousands of individual views can be called up on screen within seconds on one of the Frith internet sites, enabling people living continents away to revisit the streets of their ancestral home town, or view places in Britain where they have enjoyed holidays. Many overseas researchers welcome the chance to view special theme selections, such as transport, sports, costume and ancient monuments.

We are certain that Francis Frith would have heartily approved of these modern developments in imaging techniques, for he himself was always working at the very limits of Victorian photographic technology.

The Value of the Archive Today

Because of the benefits brought by the computer, Frith's images are increasingly studied by social historians, by researchers into genealogy and ancestory, by architects, town planners, and by teachers and schoolchildren involved in local history projects.

In addition, the archive offers every one of us an opportunity to examine the places where we and our families have lived and worked down the years. Highly successful in Frith's own era, the archive is now, a century and more on, entering a new phase of popularity.

The Past in Tune with the Future

Historians consider the Francis Frith Collection to be of prime national importance. It is the only archive of its kind remaining in private ownership and has been valued at a million pounds. However, this figure is now rapidly increasing as digital technology enables more and more people around the world to enjoy its benefits.

Francis Frith's archive is now housed in an historic timber barn in the beautiful village of Teffont in Wiltshire. Its founder would not recognize the archive office as it is today. In place of the many thousands of dusty boxes containing glass plate negatives and an all-pervading odour of photographic chemicals, there are now ranks of computer screens. He would be amazed to watch his images travelling round the world at unimaginable speeds through network and internet lines.

The archive's future is both bright and exciting. Francis Frith, with his unshakeable belief in making photographs available to the greatest number of people, would undoubtedly approve of what is being done today with his lifetime's work. His photographs, depicting our shared past, are now bringing pleasure and enlightenment to millions around the world a century and more after his death.

Carmarthenshire - *Sir Gaerfyrddin*

'THE COUNTY OF Carmarthen is 108 miles in Circumference, contains about 800,000 acres, is divided into 6 hundreds, in which are 8 Market Towns, 87 Parishes and about 5352 houses. The air is generally very good, wholesome and mild, and ye Soil not so Mountainous and steep as in other Countys, here being levels and plains, loaded with corn, & affording excellent Pasturage, having several pleasant & rich Meadows. Chief commodities are Corn, Cattle, Salmon, of ye large size Wood, Pit-Coal, & ye best Lead'.

(From Emanuel Bowen's 'Britannia Depicta', 1720.)

The above is a fine piece of evocative writing; although it was penned over two hundred and fifty years ago, it is still accurate in the broadest terms. True, boundary changes came and went; the industrial revolution barely came; and the modern trappings of life came and stayed. But fortunately, although the excesses of what is termed 'progress' arrived, they never took over from the age-old way of life. Much of the county is stuck in a time-warp, and the hardy Welsh folk carry on working 'ye land' as they did in 1720. They might have a TV and car today, but that is by choice, and for their convenience. One thing they have not done is to sell out their birthright. They are their own men (and women), initially wary of strangers and 'oft-comers', but the friendliest of any people in these British Isles.

Carmarthenshire, in Welsh Sir Gaerfyrddin, lies in south-western Wales. It is bounded on the north by the county of Cardiganshire, on the east by the county of Powys, on the south-east by the county borough of Neath and Port Talbot and the county borough of Swansea, to the south by Carmarthen Bay, and on the west by the county of Pembrokeshire.

Created on 1 April 1996, the county bears the same name and has the same boundaries as the historic county of Carmarthenshire, which existed from 1284 until 1974. Under the local government reorganisation implemented in the latter year, Carmarthenshire was incorporated into the new county of Dyfed as the districts of Carmarthen, Llanelli, and Dinefwr. The three districts were reconstituted into a county in 1996 as a result of the Local Government Act 1994, which provided for the restructuring of local administration in Wales by replacing the two-tier system of county and district councils with a single-tier system of unitary authorities.

Carmarthenshire can conjure up images of Dylan Thomas in his quiet boathouse in Laugharne, the inspiration for much of 'Under Milk Wood'; or of Sir Malcolm Campbell roaring along the flat stretches of Pendine Sands in his attempts to break the world land speed record. But one enduring picture of the county is Llanelli, at the eastern end of Carmarthen Bay, the proud home of a champion rugby team. Some people say that Llanelli has not got much going for it, but Llanelli and the people there are really warm and friendly. They are fanatical, too, about their sport, and justly so: in the 1970s, when Wales dominated the game, some of her greatest stars emerged from the town's rugby club, the 'Scarlets' of Stradey Park. Gareth Edwards, Barry John, J P R Williams ... they all started their rugby days at the pitch with the 'sospans' on the posts - these are symbols of the local tinplate industry, and subjects of the well-known rugby anthem 'Sospan Fach'.

Llanelli's nickname is Sospans because it is here where saucepans and all sorts of kitchenware are made, but of course the whole town revolves around the rugby club. Llanelli is a real working town, the product of Swansea and the valleys. And yet in direct contrast just up the road the Tywi (or Towy) flows on through fertile farmlands to Carmarthen, with all its sheep and farms. This old but lively market town has always been an important centre. Salmon and trout are chief among the tastiest delicacies associated with the county, and these can be sampled by visiting Carmarthen's covered market. Here you can find home-cured ham and organic bread, alongside delicious Carmarthenshire cheeses, such as Caws Ffermdy Cenarth, or unpasteurised Llanboidy cheese.

Between Laugharne and Pendine, on the shores of Carmarthen Bay, archaeologists made astonishing finds on the floor of Coygen Cave. The bones of extinct wild animals preserved in the stalagmites here are up to 25,000 years old. A few miles inland is Whitland (known in Welsh as Hendy-gwyn), whose history is rather more recent: this was the 10th-century meeting-place of Hywell Dda (the Good). This powerful chief drew up a code of Welsh laws that lasted over 300 years, until the English conquest in the 11th century.

Up in the remote hill country is the mysterious Llyn y Fan Fach, the lake where a beautiful fairy woman rose from the waters and married a mortal, Rhiwallon, on condition that he would not touch her with iron. Poor Rhiwallon managed to touch his wife three times - with the tip of a whip, the buckle of a glove and a ring - and she promptly disappeared into the lake, followed by her hapless husband's sheep and cattle.

One of the most romantic castle ruins in Wales is also found up in the highlands. Carreg Cennen Castle was captured in its time by the rebel leader Owain Glyndwr and by Sir Richard Herbert of Raglan, who wanted to flush out the nest of robbers hiding out there. But the dark ruins still stand, perched on a 300-foot limestone rock, and a passage still tunnels into the cliff and emerges in the old well. This ragged fortress, silhouetted against the mountains at sunset, is an unforgettable sight. Another commanding castle perched above the tranquil coast and countryside is the fortress at Llanstephan. Its rough stone walls, dating from 1192, occupy a far older hill-fort which dates from around 600BC.

By the 14th century, Carmarthen had cornered the market in wool, exporting to Flanders and beyond. The wool trade has served the county well for many centuries, and 18th-century textile machines are still on display at the museum of the Welsh woollen industry in Drefach, Felindre, near the lovely Teifi valley.

Carmarthenshire is a hilly county; its highest parts are in the east, where the Black Mountains rise. Fan Brycheiniog, rising to 2,632 feet on the border between Carmarthenshire and Powys, is the highest point. The coast has fine stretches of sandy beaches. The Brecon Beacons National Park extends into the east of the county, covering over 87 square miles. The main river is the Towy, which rises in the Cambrian Mountains in Powys, and runs through the town of Carmarthen on its way to Carmarthen Bay. The valley of the Towy is a fertile tract some thirty miles long and two miles wide in the midst of a wild and rugged region. It crosses the county from north-east to south-west, and is the largest valley in the county. The hills that rise on either side are beautifully wooded or richly grassed.

The valley contains the market towns of Llandeilo and Llandovery, while the port of Carmarthen commands all the traffic through the fertile land around the head of the estuary. The prettiest portion is from six or so miles north of Llandovery, but between that tract and the mouth of the river there is much to delight the eye, especially when the valley is viewed from its bordering heights. By reason of the breadth and flatness of the lower part of the valley, the prospect suffers when the viewpoint is at a low level. As is usual in rivers where the valley is flat, the stream meanders in wide sweeping curves; these are seen to advantage from the old Dynevor

Castle and from the Dryslwyn Castle hill.

The vale of Towy has been called 'the heart of South Wales'. It is famous in Welsh life, Welsh history and Welsh song. In the days of the Welsh princes, it was the political centre of the southern kingdom, and, save Glamorgan, it was the most distinguished strip of south Wales. The river that runs through the valley has been 'celebrated for all time for the sewin (a type of sea trout) that begin to run in the first July floods'. As in the Usk, Wye and Teifi, fish run up it freely, travelling far into the mountain gorges. It is partly preserved, but permission to fish in certain areas can be obtained.

Other rivers of the county are the Taff, which crosses the south-western part of the county and reaches the sea at Laugharne; the Gwendraeth, which enters Carmarthen Bay at Kidwelly; and the Loughor, which flows from the Black Mountains to Loughor, forming part of the boundary between Carmarthenshire and the county of Swansea.

The climate is moderate. The winters are mild and the summers warm, but it is a wet county with an annual rainfall of 40 to 60 inches. The population of the county is about 169,000, with a high proportion of the population fluent in the Welsh, and the county was slow to relinquish traditional costumes. Carmarthen was, according to legend, the birthplace of Merlin, the Celtic magician and counsellor to King Arthur. The main towns are Llanelli (population 42,000), which is the administrative centre of the unitary authority, Carmarthen (14,600), and Ammanford (8,100). There is a Crown Court in Carmarthen, and the police authority is the Dyfed-Powys Police, which has its headquarters in Carmarthen.

The main industry in the county is agriculture. Sheep and hardy cattle are raised in the mountains and valleys of the north, and dairy farming is carried out in the Vale of Towy. Salmon fishing on the Towy, which used to be of importance, has declined. Anthracite and hard coal are mined north of Llanelli, on the extension of the south Wales coalfield. The mine at Betws near Ammanford was privatised in 1994. With the decline of the coal industry, Llanelli is having to diversify into the manufacture of bathroom and household goods, beer, chemicals, plastics, rubber vehicle parts, piano and organ keyboards, and women's clothing; the aerospace industry also has a base in the town.

There are numerous relics in Carmarthenshire of prehistoric and Roman occupation. The Romans built roads and a fortification called Maridunum, which later became known as Caerfyrddin, and eventually Carmarthen. The Normans arrived in 1080, and built castles at Carmarthen, Kidwelly, Llanstephan, and Laugharne. Edward I of England created the county of Carmarthenshire in 1284, and its boundaries were extended under Henry VIII. In

the meantime it had become the Welsh centre of the wool trade. The people of the county were strong supporters of the nationalist leader Owen Glendower (Owain Glyndwr) at the time of his rebellion against English rule at the beginning of the 15th century. It was at Abergwili that Bishop Richard Davies produced the first translation into Welsh of the Bible and the Prayer Book, and religious revivals in the 17th and 18th centuries originated in the county. The Vicar of Llanddowror, Griffith Jones, was the founder of the Welsh circulating charity schools. In the mid 19th century, Carmarthenshire was closely involved in the Rebecca Riots, which were a response to economic recession and the high road tolls that discouraged trade. Beginning in 1839, men dressed as women attacked the tollbooths that collected the money from road users. The disturbances finally came to a halt in 1844.

Carmarthen was the site of a Roman amphitheatre. A short distance from the town of Llandeilo are Cam Goch, an Iron Age hill fort, and Carreg Cennen Castle, a fortress built in the 14th century on a cliff edge. East of Carmarthen is Paxton's Tower, built as a memorial to Nelson in 1811. Five miles south-west of Llandovery, at Llanwrda, visitors may see the Dolaucothi Gold Mines, which were exploited by the Celts and Romans some 2,000 years ago, and were last worked in 1938. There are excellent beaches to the east and to the west of the Towy estuary. The poet Dylan Thomas lived for many years in Laugharne and is buried there.

Our tour of this unique county begins close to where the M4 motorway enters the county from Swansea. It then takes a clockwise bearing, as far as possible, around the border, but obviously has to divert into the central parts - like Carmarthen itself - before leaving the county at Brynamman, close to the entry point at Loughor. Please note that depending on which map or guide book you have, the River Towy (the English spelling) is often spelt the Welsh way, 'Tywi'. Even more confusing is that the River Taff often drops one f to become the 'Taf'.

LOUGHOR
The Cross c 1955 L466017
Loughor, the starting point for this Carmarthenshire tour, is
not actually in the county; it is separated from it by the river
Loughor, and is on the outskirts of Swansea. The market cross
stood in this position until it had to make way for progress in
the form of the motor car. Having said that, a rather nice
Vauxhall is to be seen outside the general store.

LOUGHOR, THE BRIDGE 1936 87746

A double-decker bus can be seen crossing the Iron Bridge, which spans the river Loughor close to its estuary. In the background is the industrialised shoreline leading to Llanelli. It is a pity that the pace of modern life makes so many visitors miss Loughor Castle; its present situation alongside the busy A484 road means that unless one is actively hunting for this fine medieval castle, attention will be focused on the traffic and bridge ahead.

LLWYNHENDY, THE VILLAGE 1936 87748

On entering the county of Carmarthenshire, the unprepossessing village shown here is the first place on the itinerary. The time when this picture was taken was obviously a transitional one between trams and motor vehicles, as the road is nicely tarmaced with no sign of tramlines. However, on the poles along the road are the electrical conductors needed by the trams which, no doubt, were soon to be demolished.

LLWYNHENDY, GENERAL VIEW 1936 87749

As we look across toward the village, we can see that the land is rough scrubland, nothing like the fertile valleys which the visitor will come to know. This is largely because this area, being close to Llanelli, was sitting on a bed of pure anthracite coal, which stunted the growth of vegetation. On the right-hand side near the skyline is the village's small Baptist chapel.

LLWYNHENDY, SOAR BAPTIST CHAPEL 1936 87750

The Baptist chapel, now seen here in close-up, is Soar Chapel, which was built in 1850 and then again rebuilt and enlarged in 1868. Although Llwynhendy is only a tiny hamlet, the chapel certainly has a large graveyard with some sizeable headstones and tombs.

LLWYNHENDY, HIGH STREET c1955 L276003

Both the tramlines and the conductors have now disappeared in this later photograph; but although we are now well into the age of the motor car, there is little traffic to be seen. In fact, there is virtually no more traffic after twenty years since the 1936 picture (87748).

LLANELLI, FROM STRADEY WOODS 1957 L73049

Today the view is quiet and smoke-free, but this was not always the case; Llanelli was once the tin plate capital of the world. A forest of tall chimneys flung a pall of lucrative smoke over the town. The boisterous song of 'Sospan Fach' (which means 'the little saucepan') was Llanelli's theme tune.

LLANELLI, STEPNEY STREET c1960 L73055

LLANELLI
Stepney Street c1960
The new-found cleanliness following the demise of the tin plate industry can be seen here. Lloyds Bank, just visible on the left, faces a parade of different shops, and the size of Paige's department store at the corner of Vaughan Street indicates that new sources of wealth had been tapped.

LLANELLI
Parc Howard c1955
Through the generosity of Sir Stafford and Lady Howard, the inhabitants of Llanelli are in possession of Bryncaerau Castle and the park, which covers about twenty-five acres.

LLANELLI, PARC HOWARD c1955 L73059

LLANELLI, PARC HOWARD c1955 L73060

The park, now Parc Howard, has been laid out for leisure activities with a children's paddling pool, while the mansion has been converted into a museum and refreshment rooms. A little way from the mansion are the exotic botanical gardens, which we can see here.

LLANELLI, PARC HOWARD c1955 L73066

The ancient stone circle at the farthest point is associated with the bards, and the tradition of the Gorsedd or Eisteddfod was incorporated into the general landscape. Across the small valley is a pleasant mixture of modern semi-detached and older terraced houses.

LLANELLI, TOWN HALL SQUARE 1957 L73063
Llanelli is still very much alive, and Town Hall Square is laid out in a most symmetrical and pleasing manner. It possesses a rather grand neo-Jacobean Town Hall with a highly decorative clock tower.

LLANELLI, SWISS VALLEY c1960 L73073
The higher rainfall and the natural lakes of Wales have always been necessary to meet the water requirements of England. This view of the Swiss Valley, however, shows not a natural lake but a beautiful drowned basin, which now supplies the West Midlands with its precious natural resource.

LLANELLI, THE CHURCH c1965 L73097

The centre of the town, shown here, is certainly becoming the domain of the motorist; we can see few vehicles, but a plethora of road signs. A rather nice Mark 1 Cortina can be seen passing the Norman parish church on the left. The large trees in front of the church do not permit much more speculation about the architecture. However, the Mansel Hotel on the extreme left is most conveniently situated for wedding receptions.

BURRY PORT, THE VILLAGE c1965 B472012

This general view shows typical houses of the time; the terrace in the foreground is followed by 1950s semis leading down to the waters of the inlet of Carmarthen Bay, with the Gower peninsular just visible in the far background.

BURRY PORT, THE GOLF LINKS c1965 B472025

Whilst Cardiff and Llanelli were, and always will be, the home of Rugby Union, golfing was the Welshman's second love - although in this picture no one was playing, at least not on this tee. With Burry Port being so close to the sea, the all-year-round golfers would have to be a hardy lot to withstand the wild and windy weather.

BURRY PORT, THE HARBOUR c1960 B472039

Burry Port looks and, for the most part, is indeed a tranquil spot for pleasure boating. The local yachtsmen, however, are familiar with the complex channels of the Burry estuary and the dangerous Cefn Sidan sands, which have caught many a visitor unawares.

BURRY PORT, THE STATION AND STATION ROAD C1955 B472036
The pride of the stationmaster at Burry Port is typical of the time - it was considered the stationmaster's duty to make the platform as attractive as possible. This can be seen clearly in the rockery and floral arrangements shown here. The railway line west of Llanelli was the creation of the great days of the coal and tin plate trade.

BURRY PORT, THE HARBOUR c1965 B472061

BURRY PORT
The Harbour c1965
The little harbour of Burry Port was in times past a busy export terminal for tin and fine anthracite coal. Those days are over; the small port, dominated by a big power station seen on the far right, now serves as a pleasant boat marina.

◆

BURRY PORT
Station Road c1960
The road rises gently before swinging to the left into the station yard. The pleasant sunshine seems to have forced the owner of the shop on the right to lower the blinds. However, the absence of any signboard would suggest that it was unoccupied. George Mason next door is 'open all hours' for business, and the bicycle stands ready to make its next delivery.

BURRY PORT, STATION ROAD c1960 B472059

PEMBREY
The Links 1936

Pembrey, like its close neighbour Burry Port, always had an active golfing fraternity. There is not much activity on the links on the day this photograph was taken - so we might assume the golfers were slaking their thirst at the nineteenth hole.

◆

PEMBREY
St Illtyd's Church 1936

The oldest building in the area is Pembrey Church, St Illtyd's. The tower is Norman and the roof 16th-century. Here there is a monument to a French soldier, Colonel Coquilin, and his daughter Adeline. They were drowned when their ship, the 'Jenne Emma', struck the Cefn Sidan sands. The inscription states that Adeline was 'the niece of Josephine, consort to the renowned individual Napoleon Bonaparte'.

PEMBREY, THE LINKS 1936 87818

PEMBREY, ST ILLTYD'S CHURCH 1936 87819

PEMBREY, LLANDO TERRACE C1955 P202044
The corner shop on the immediate left distinguishes Llando Terrace. From the partial billboard on the gable end, it was obviously a retailer of the News of the World, which at this date, it may be interesting to recall, was a working class but quite serious broadsheet, and not the sensational tabloid of today.

KIDWELLY, THE CASTLE AND THE CHURCH 1893 32802
The sweeping bend in the river Towy leads the eye past the castle to the church in the background. Kidwelly lies due south of Carmarthen. The borough is one of the oldest in the principality; it received its first Charter under Henry VIII.

KIDWELLY, THE CASTLE 1925 77317

KIDWELLY
The Castle 1925

The town is chiefly noteworthy for its noble old castle, the remains of which have been carefully strengthened so that the relic is the best preserved of the nine castles in Carmarthenshire. It was originally founded in the time of Henry I, and later additions were made in the reign of Edward II.

◆

KIDWELLY
The Church 1925

The church was dedicated to St Mary the Virgin during the Norman period; it had belonged to a former Benedictine priory founded by Roger, Bishop of Salisbury. It is one of the few monastic churches in the county; these were preserved in the violent suppression of the monasteries and permitted to remain to be used as the parish church.

KIDWELLY, THE CHURCH 1925 77319

KIDWELLY, THE WAR MEMORIAL 1925 77320

KIDWELLY, VIEW FROM THE CASTLE c1960 K17038
The four round towers of the castle which enclose the courtyard can be climbed to a considerable height. At that elevation, the views encompass the surrounding countryside; in this scene, we can see across the river to a development of modern semi-detached houses, which would be newly-built at this time.

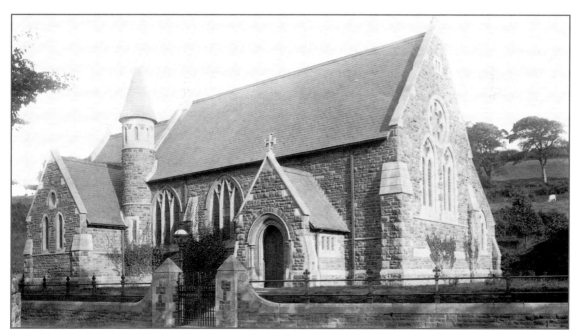

FERRYSIDE, THE CHURCH 1893 32789
One mile to the south of Ferryside is the church, the old 13th-century church of St Ismael, perched on a high promontory above the railway and the sands. Like all churches, it has undergone many changes and architectural additions which belie its real age.

FERRYSIDE
The Coast and the Village 1925

The village stands on the east side of the Towy where the river breaks out to sea through a widespread expanse of sandbanks at low tide. This can be partially seen here; the spits are appearing, indicating that the tide is on the ebb.

FERRYSIDE
Coastal View 1925
As we look down onto Ferryside, we can see the main railway line to Carmarthen at the very right-hand side. The line curves along the foreshore of the river Towy, giving passengers a fine view of Llanstephan Castle on the opposite western bank, seen here in the far background.

FERRYSIDE, THE COAST AND THE VILLAGE 1925 77305

FERRYSIDE, COASTAL VIEW 1925 77307

FERRYSIDE, THE BEACH AND THE LIFEBOAT HOUSE 1937 88153

The lifeboat house was deemed necessary by the local authorities in view of the dangerous channels and sandbanks already noted. Many small craft, both working fishing boats and pleasure vessels, regularly experienced difficulties. The lifeboat crew, pictured here, seem to have their priorities right in simply taking the sun rather than attempting repairs to the boat in the foreground!

FERRYSIDE, THE VILLAGE 1937 88154

This photograph shows the terminus for the day trips to London by bus. Some enterprising individual at the café ensured that waiting passengers were well looked after: not only teas were provided, but billiards as well!

FERRYSIDE
THE COAST AND A BOATMAN 1925
77309
The man seen pushing off from the shore here, his sizeable skiff equipped with both sails and outboard engine, is no fisherman. By the look of the boarding plank and the amount of seating, he is more likely to be a ferryman. He would need both sources of power to manoeuvre across the dangerous currents of the River Towy whilst carrying his passengers across from Ferryside to Llanstephan.

FERRYSIDE, THE GLAN TYWI ESTATE c1955 F20032

As we move further away from the industrialised regions, the equable climate and fertility of the soil begin to show themselves in the lush meadows and woodland. In the foreground is the recently-built council estate: as with all such estates, owing to financial considerations, the houses were all identical. Over to the left of the picture can be seen the railway line heading north to Carmarthen.

FERRYSIDE, THE BEACH c1960 F20037

Here we can see a closer view of the railway line, which runs parallel to the river virtually all the way to Carmarthen. Since it is tidal at this point, the Towy has a nice wide beach for all kinds of activities for young and old. The rocks in the foreground seem to be the domain of the older generation, whilst the children in the distance make their own pleasures in the sand and water.

FERRYSIDE, VIEW OF LLANSTEPHAN C1965 F20070
Looking across the mighty Towy, we can pick out the ruined castle on the hillside to the far left. On this side of the river, and pulled well clear, is evidence of boating and fishing activity. The craft closer to the water is a twin-hulled catamaran, and more likely to be used purely for pleasure.

CARMARTHEN, ON THE RIVER 1890 28126
Carmarthen stands on rising ground on the north side of the Towy. The site was occupied by the Roman settlement of Maridunum, meaning 'sea fort'; the word Carmarthen is the Celtic equivalent of this.

CARMARTHEN, THE RIVERSIDE 1893 32772

A popular promenade on the river Towy is an embankment, called the Bulwark, extending for about a mile on the south side of the river. There is a similar walk on the north bank, and on summer evenings there are many pleasure boats on the water. This picture was obviously not a summer evening!

CARMARTHEN, ST PETER'S CHURCH 1925 77296

At the east end of Spilman Street is St Peter's Church, an old building on the highest ground in the older portion of the town. Little is known about this church, including the date of its erection. However, the earliest reference to the building is in a document in the time of Henry I, who reigned from 1100 to 1135.

CARMARTHEN, THE TOWN HALL 1893 32780
This large and imposing building complete with clock tower, built in something of a Victorian neo-Gothic style, was home to the Town Council and associated bodies. It is still the age of the horse, though none can be seen - the roadway immediately in the foreground appears to need some attention. It is interesting to note that the blinds of the shops on the left are of the old-fashioned type which needed metal supports.

CARMARTHEN, GUILD HALL STREET 1925 77284
There are several major changes in this picture compared with No 32780. We are looking along Guild Hall Street towards what was previously called the Town Hall. The street has now been tarmaced and early motor vehicles have appeared. Additionally, two of the three shops on the left have now gained self-supporting roller blinds, whilst the furthest away still rests on its stilts. Driving was not the stress that it is today - it is crucial that the owner of the open-topped car notices the little boy only inches behind his rear wheel!

CARMARTHEN, CORACLES 1898 41093
This picture was obviously taken in the fishing season, where coracles were used for their convenience. These boats were used by the ancient Britons, and are still made in the traditional way: canvas is stretched on a framework of interwoven rods and rendered waterproof with pitch or tar.

CARMARTHEN, THE TRAINING COLLEGE 1906 53735

This college is the second-oldest institution of higher education in Wales: it was founded in 1848 to train teachers for Church schools. It is an institution where the two languages of Welsh and English are given equal status and respect.

CARMARTHEN, THE RECREATION GROUND 1910 62619

In early days the hub of the community was the church, but later, as we see here, it was the neighbourhood recreation ground. Beyond the terrace of houses, two crescents converge through landscaped gardens and woodland to the central bandstand. This would be used to shelter the public from a sudden shower, and it was also a place where the local band would play on occasions. Dominating the scene behind the other leisure activities is the splendid rugby pitch - Rugby Union, of course!

CARMARTHEN, GENERAL VIEW 1910 62620
Despite being hemmed in by the surrounding hills, by the turn of the century Carmarthen was already a sizeable and bustling town. Unlike many other Welsh towns, whose growth was based on coal or iron and steel, Carmarthen had long been a market town and the centre for an age-old agricultural tradition. On both sides of the main street are dwellings of all shapes, sizes and ages, including a fine mock-Tudor gabled residence in the near left.

CARMARTHEN, GUILDHALL SQUARE 1925 77283
Guildhall Square contains the Assize Court, the Town Council Chamber and the Magistrates' Clerk's Office. Nott Square leads down to the Guildhall and Law Courts, with the South African War Memorial in front of the classical and dignified Guildhall facade.

CARMARTHEN
LAMMAS STREET 1925 77287
This is Carmarthen's longest and widest thoroughfare. Lammas Street contains the Crimean War Memorial to the Royal Welsh Fusiliers. The proximity of the Drover's Arms Inn on the left indicates that this part of the street held the cattle market in bygone days.

CARMARTHEN, LAMMAS STREET 1893 32781
This older photograph of the wide and almost empty Lammas Street shows the Crimean War Memorial in the centre. There is little activity, and a horse-drawn carriage seems to be almost abandoned in the foreground.

CARMARTHEN, LAMMAS STREET c1955 C31032
The War Memorial still stands proudly in the centre of the street, although we are getting very up to date here. Double-decker buses of the style seen on the right are still used today, and there is a garage on both sides of the road, both of which are AA registered. The only sense of antiquity is that the milk is carried in churns and not the tankers of today.

CARMARTHEN, THE GENERAL SIR WILLIAM NOTT STATUE 1925 77289
Carmarthen had a taste for memorials and statues, especially if they had a military connection. The statue of General Sir William Nott, who played a gallantly obscure part in the Afghan Wars, stands before the castle gateway.

CARMARTHEN, THE WAR MEMORIAL AND THE INFIRMARY 1925 77291
Yet another War Memorial stands proudly in front of the modern facade of the Infirmary; the inscription tells us that it is dedicated to 'The Immortal Memory of the Men of Carmarthenshire who fell at the Great War 1914 - 1918'.

CARMARTHEN, THE COUNTY SCHOOL AND THE GRAMMAR SCHOOL 1925 77295
The two schools are conveniently situated side by side, each catering to its own academic level. Whatever the academic attributes of a school were, sporting activities were always high on the agenda in Wales. This is demonstrated admirably in this shot, which shows the neatly manicured grass tennis courts.

CARMARTHEN, ST DAVID'S CHURCH 1925 77299
Lammas Street is the main thoroughfare of Carmarthen, and it will come as no surprise that there are several churches along this way. Two are facing each other on either side of the street, one of which is the originally Norman edifice of St David's. However, looking towards the church, it is the overgrown nature of the churchyard which is most noticeable - the grasses are in many cases higher than the headstones.

CARMARTHEN, FROM PENYMORFA 1933 85597

This is a well-chosen vantage point to give the viewer a distant view of Carmarthen across the River Towy. You will note that a black sedan motor car has pulled into the small lay-by to admire the view before continuing its ascent up the hill.

CARMARTHEN, THE RIVER TOWY 1933 85600

Here we see a peaceful view of the River Towy on a quiet day, with no sign of any people or indeed of any activity whatsoever. The five small fishing smacks moored in the river and not at work indicate that this could well be a Sunday, when all good Welshmen honour their day of rest at the local chapel.

CARMARTHEN, MERLIN'S OAK 1936 87418
The wizard's oak stood near the town for hundreds of years. Its stump was eventually shored up with concrete, because Merlin had warned that 'when the oak falls down, then falls the town'.

CARMARTHEN, MERLIN'S OAK c1965 C31130
The progressing traffic congestion, which boomed in the 1950s and 1960s, won out in the end, and poor Merlin's Oak's remains were moved gingerly to the town museum.

CARMARTHEN, THE BROADCAST HALL, TRINITY COLLEGE c1955
C31008

CARMARTHEN
The Broadcast Hall, Trinity College c1955
This scene shows the more modern buildings of Trinity College, which is the new name for the teacher training institution. It has extended its range of courses dramatically, so that in addition to teacher training, it now also offers BA and BSc degrees, many of them of an innovative nature, such as broadcasting.

◆

CARMARTHEN
Coracle Fishing on the Towy c1955
Coracle men fish in pairs. They stretch the net between them, and when they feel a fish struggling in the meshes each hauls in his end. There is no dress code, but the fisherman on the right looks better equipped for going out to dinner.

CARMARTHEN, CORACLE FISHING ON THE TOWY c1955 C31031

CARMARTHEN, THE CORACLE MAN c1955 C31033
This photograph should really have been called 'Man with Coracle' rather than 'Coracle Man', as he has something of a resemblance to an upright and overgrown tortoise. The serious point is, however, that the coracles, as well as being virtually unsinkable, are so light that they can be easily carried.

CARMARTHEN, KING STREET c1955 C31060

The people of Carmarthen certainly had plenty of choice of footwear in the High Street: the shop on the immediate left is offering not only the long-gone Lotus shoes, but the still-surviving Kay shoes as well. Boots the Chemist also have a store just along from the shoe shop.

CARMARTHEN, THE HORSE FAIR c1950 C31086

Carmarthen's horse fairs were the Welsh equivalent of the Appleby fairs in Cumbria, and were still being held as late as 1955. Markets and fairs are not new to the town, as a Charter of Henry VIII gave the innkeepers the right to open all day on the five market days. This practice has made Carmarthen a relaxed and happy town!

CARMARTHEN, BANC Y FELIN, THE VILLAGE c1960 C31112
This picturesque village photograph is undated, but with the approaching car keeping well to the centre of the road we must be in the 1950s or 1960s. The Esso sign always meant 'happy motoring', and this would certainly be true on quiet roads like this. The road sign in the foreground indicates that the next left is to Llanstephan, among other places.

CARMARTHEN, LAMMAS STREET c1965 C31116
Further along Lammas Street is the obelisk in commemoration of Sir Thomas Picton, who fell at Waterloo. In recent years the top of the monument has been removed, which gives it a stumpy appearance. Has Carmarthen lost its taste for military commemoration?

CARMARTHEN
THE GUILDHALL c1965 C31121
The old town has undergone a certain amount of rebuilding behind Guildhall Square. The market has gone, although the attractive old clock tower has been retained. The motorcar is once again becoming a problem, even in the market towns of Wales, as we can see from the traffic island and traffic lights.

CARMARTHEN, DARK GATES C1965 C31128

There were three 'Dark Gates' in Carmarthen: these were simply narrow streets that linked the Market Place to Lammas Street. Much more interesting, though, is the policeman on traffic duty, once again illustrating the approach of traffic congestion. With the traffic lights controlling the main roads, the policeman at first glance seems superfluous; but it appears that the powers that be had not seen a need for a traffic light at the bottom of the Dark Gate.

CARMARTHEN, COUNTY HALL C1965 C31143

The old bridge over the river Towy has now been replaced by a new concrete one, and little remains of the castle beyond the gatehouse. The site, once the strong point of royal power in south-west Wales, is now occupied by the County Hall with its high slate roof, which dominates the view of Carmarthen from the river.

CARMARTHEN, THE RIVERSIDE c1965 C31144

It is hard to imagine that this serene view is only yards away from the hustle and bustle of the town centre. Across the river, the rear of County Hall dominates the skyline; the keen eye can see that one of the riverside buildings is the Carmarthen Farmers Co-operative Society Limited.

CARMARTHEN, HORSE SHOE BEND, THE RIVER TOWY c1965 C31145

This panorama shows the town in the valley of the Towy but already expanding up the hillsides. The river at its first right-hand bend will soon break through the low-lying land to redirect itself and form a natural feature known as a horse shoe or ox bow lake.

LLANSTEPHAN, THE CASTLE 1893 32794

The shell of Llanstephan Castle sits on the summit of a precipitous hill, the base of which is directly on the beach. Not only is the castle suffering from the ravages of time, but also its base is being rapidly eroded by the twice-daily tides of the sea.

There are two villages opposite each other on the estuary of the Towy: Ferryside and Llanstephan, once again famous for its ruined castle. There is a pretty cliff walk around the castle hill to St Anthony's Well; a little like Lourdes, the well formerly had a reputation for miraculous properties.

LLANSTEPHAN, THE CASTLE 1893 32798

LLANSTEPHAN, THE VILLAGE 1933 85595
This is a very scenic and small village which lies between the Towy and Taf estuaries at the point where the Towy, the Gwendraeth and the Taf flow into Carmarthen Bay. Its impressive castle above the village and the elegant mansion of Plas Llanstephan overlook the Towy estuary.

LLANSTEPHAN, THE ROAD TO THE BEACH 1933 85596
A tree-lined avenue leads down this pleasant stretch of road to the small beach at Llanstephan. A lone figure meanders along towards a bend in the road; by virtue of his being on his own, he is probably local to the area.

LLANSTEPHAN, THE COTTAGE PRIVATE HOTEL c1960 L529026

LLANSTEPHAN
The Cottage Private Hotel c1960
This small hotel certainly lives up to its name of 'private', sitting as it does in its secluded situation. It would appeal to those who simply wanted to get away from it all. Although it would be within easy walking distance of the beach, the visitors might prefer to contemplate the idyllic views extending to the rural farmland.

ST CLEARS
St Mary's Church c1955
To give it its full title, this view is of St Mary Magdalen's Church. The walls of the church show a tendency to lean outwards, but it contains some strong Norman work. It is a great shame that financial constraints of these times have necessitated re-roofing this fine building with cheap slates.

ST CLEARS, ST MARY'S CHURCH c1955 S432005

St Clears, St Mary's Church, Interior c1955 S432044
Inside St Mary Magdalen's church we can clearly see the fine chancel arch leading to the altar. Although a very small church, it has played a central role over the centuries in the continuity of community spirit.

LAUGHARNE, THE BOAT HOUSE c1955 L250046

This attractive boat house is set at the foot of a steep cliff alongside the River Taf with its 'heron-priested' shore. The poet Dylan Thomas lived here for the last four years of his life. The view he enjoyed from its windows is magnificent and inspired him to write many of his most famous poems. In Laugharne he also wrote 'Under Milk Wood', the play about Llareggub, his fictitious name for the town. The boat house is now a heritage centre dedicated to he poet.

LAUGHARNE, THE CASTLE c1955 L250015

Laugharne is an old borough teeming with interest for those with antiquarian tastes. Its setting is exquisite, nestling between Llanstephan and Pendine. The castle, here seen shrouded with creeper, offers fine views over the broad estuary where oyster catchers call plaintively from the distant sandbanks.

LAUGHARNE, THE CASTLE c1955 L250013

The ruinous Welsh coastal fortress, with its two gatehouses, was converted to an Elizabethan mansion by Sir John Perrot, the tenancy being granted to him by Elizabeth I. Unfortunately, Sir John was sent to the Tower and his house with its fine glass and furnishings went into gradual decline. It stayed ruinous until the 1930s when it was restored. The writer Richard Hughes, author of 'High Wind in Jamaica', lived in it for some years.

LAUGHARNE, ST MARTIN'S CHURCH c1965 L250064

Ancient customs linger in the borough, including 'beating the bounds'; local government also smacks of bygone days, as it is conducted by a portreeve - an officer junior to the mayor - and a jury of 13 members.

PENDINE, THE CAVES c1955 P205010

The seaside village of Pendine is situated on the west side of the united estuaries of the Tywi and Taf. It was, and is, a pleasant holiday spot for Carmarthen people and tourists alike. As we can see, the sand was firm enough for the visitors to bring their cars onto it, and the sea-eroded caves held many delights for the youngsters.

PENDINE, THE BEACH c1955 P205030

The sands at Pendine are five miles long at low tide and a splendid place for pilgrimage for motor enthusiasts. The great names of pre-second World War racing all tried their luck here, including Sir Malcolm Campbell. But for Welshmen, the sands are forever associated with J G Parry Thomas, the only man who held the World Speed Record. Later he was tragically killed when his car 'Babs' skidded on the wet sands.

PENDINE, THE BEACH c1955 P205043

This general view of the village shows its sheltered position from the northerly winds. The houses are scattered down the hillside, and come in all shapes and sizes from large detached villas to small terraced houses. There were no car parking problems in those days, as the cars simply pulled up against the sea wall. Although the sands were firm and dry at low tide, the high sea wall was a necessary protection from the very high spring tides.

PENDINE, THE ROCKS c1955 P205044

The outcrops of mainly granite rocks make a majestic backdrop to the beach. The constant rock falls formed many fascinating rock pools, and the blowholes caused by the battering of the sea formed natural caves, some of which tunnelled deep into the cliff.

PENDINE, THE ROCKS AND THE CAVES c1955 P205049

PENDINE
The Rocks and the Caves c1955

Here we can see a closer view of the myriad shapes and sizes of nature's work. But the scene also shows how safe the beach was for even the youngest of the young. A vigilant father watches with absent-minded concern as his little daughter takes her first faltering steps.

CENARTH
Coracle Fishing c1955

Cenarth, or Kenarth as it is often spelled, is situated alongside the river and the Cardiganshire border; here the ancient coracle is still in regular use for the salmon fishing. The men worked in pairs a few yards apart, as we have seen, and speedily lifted the net at the slightest movement of a salmon. If you look carefully, you can see that the net has just been lifted here.

CENARTH, CORACLE FISHING c1955 C376009

CENARTH, CORACLE FISHING c1955 C376011

Coracles are little oval boats, made of wooden frames covered with leather and pitch. They were probably used by Stone Age fishermen, and craftsmen still produce them at Cenarth's Coracle Centre. This also houses the National Coracle Museum, which has a wonderful collection of coracles from all over the world - including Vietnam, North America, Tibet, India and Iraq.

CENARTH, SHEEP DIPPING c1965 C376039

The men of Cenarth were not ones to waste time on disinfectant by using the more traditional sheep dip as seen in England. The sheep were simply driven down to the river to await their fate.

CENARTH
SHEEP DIPPING c1960 C376034
The drovers and dogs would drive the sheep into the river, forcing them to swim to the other side and thus get a thoroughly good dipping. They valued their sheep - the coracle men took to the river to ensure they all got across safely.

NEWCASTLE EMLYN, THE BRIDGE c1955 N118042

The small overgrown bridge here carries the road over the river Teifi before leading into the town itself. The 'new' castle, from which the town takes its name, was built in the 13th century by the Welsh, but it subsequently passed into English hands - this is a nice turn of phrase, but one can assume that the Welsh put up a fight.

NEWCASTLE EMLYN, GENERAL VIEW c1955 N118048

Nestling deep in a wooded valley, Newcastle Emlyn is less picturesque than other spots in the county. The town had the first printing press in Wales, which was set up here in 1718.

NEWCASTLE EMLYN, SYCAMORE STREET c1955 N118051

There is no political correctness shown here - the Senior Service cigarettes sold at the first shop have the most striking sign of the street. Next door, Mr James has a good display of ironmongery; as can be seen beneath his name, he dealt in farm implements of all shapes and sizes.

NEWCASTLE EMLYN, THE CLOCK TOWER c1955 N118055

The town itself consists basically of one curving main street, with pleasant 19th-century houses and the market hall with a clock tower. Newcastle Emlyn comes to life on Fair days, as it is the sales centre for the cattle and sheep of a wide surrounding area of farmland.

NEWCASTLE EMLYN, LLOYD'S TERRACE c1955 N118052

At first glance, this street would appear to be simply a row of terraced houses; but look beneath the surface, and you will note how times have changed. Every house has its own identity, from pebble-dash through brick to stucco, and there is even just one with bay windows. The Morris 1000 has to park on the street - today, every house would have its own garage.

NEWCASTLE EMLYN, MAIN STREET c1955 N118054

The omnipresent Morris 1000 can park with a clear conscience, as these are the days long before yellow lines of any description. Halfway down Main Street we can see the clean facade of Lloyds Bank; although it would be far-fetched to contemplate a bank robbery in Newcastle Emlyn, this bank branch would not be a good choice, as the Police Station is immediately adjacent.

FELINDRE, THE VILLAGE C1960 F208009

A rough-hewn hump-backed bridge leads in to this sleepy hamlet. The photograph was taken in high summer - the lowered sash windows indicate a seasonally hot day, but obviously not hot enough to deter the youngster from riding his bicycle.

FELINDRE, GENERAL VIEW C1960 F208010

To assume that this area was always tranquil is an error of judgement, as forty mills once clustered around Felindre; in its heyday it was known as 'the Huddersfield of Wales'. Today the mills have gone, but a nearby museum tells the story of this community, which was dependant for its livelihood on spinning and weaving and forgotten skills of old.

PENCADER
Main Road c1955 P204006
As the main road winds gently up into the village,
we can see its history old and new, side by side. The
horse and cart on the left could have been from a
century before, whereas directly across the road is a
tiny filling station and a modern telephone box.

PENCADER, HIGH STREET c1955 P204009

A closer view of the filling station shows it to be a purveyor of the Esso brand. Between the petrol pumps and the telephone kiosk is the local Post Office. It is more than likely that the postmaster or mistress fulfilled the dual role of dispensing pensions and petrol.

PENCADER, THE SQUARE c1955 P204010

Whatever the size of the town or village in Wales generally, and in Carmarthenshire in particular, each place had its Market Square, which was usually the focal point of the community. The Welsh also had a great affinity with statues; the one here overlooking the Square commemorates the local men who fell in the Great War.

PENCADER, THE VILLAGE C1955 P204019

LLANYBYDDER, THE RIVER C1960 L205003

PENCADER
The Village c1955

After passing through the Market Square, the road drops away quite steeply; but we can note on the right that Pencader catered for tourists, as we can see a sign immediately behind the telegraph pole saying 'Vacancy'. Further down the hill, in the halcyon days before the supermarkets ruled, a van makes its delivery to the local store.

LLANYBYDDER
The River c1960

As we approach this small market centre we see a great loop of the river Teifi, with the moorland of Llanybydder Mountain (also known as Llanybyther) in the far distance. The Teifi is wide and slow-moving at this point, and thus ideal for trout and salmon fishing.

LLANYBYDDER, THE SQUARE 1949 L205007

Llanybydder's present fame, not only in Wales but in England as well, rests on its Horse Fair, which is now the largest in Britain. On the last Thursday of every month the town gives itself over to the horse, and the scene can only be matched in some of the country towns of Ireland where Horse Fairs still flourish. This picture was obviously not taken on a Thursday!

LLANYBYDDER, GENERAL VIEW c1960 L205013

The fertile soils and moist climate around the town are well-shown here by the large amount of deciduous tree growth. Most of the houses appear to have a stucco finish, and will be well protected by the prolific planting of the conifers in the foreground.

LLANYBYDDER, VIEW FROM HIGHMEAD c1960 L205019
As we look out over this beautiful vista, we can see the lush growth and greenery in the foreground; but as the moorland ascends in the background, there begins to be a lack of growth above the tree line.

LLANYBYDDER, THE POST OFFICE 1949 L205023
The road sign in the foreground is a quaint piece of post-war history: the 'major road ahead' is a relative term, as there is no sign of traffic on either road. The post office stands proudly on the junction.

LLANYBYDDER
THE CROSS ROADS 1949 L205024
This photograph was obviously taken in very close proximity
to No L205023, as the post office is now on the left. The
'major road' can be clearly seen, totally void of traffic. Across
the road from the post office stands a public house, which
obviously has connections with the famous horse fairs - a
horse is pictured on the pub sign.

LLANWRDA, THE OLD FARM c1960
L271007
The Frith photographer surely captured this scene to illustrate the extravagant and idyllic beauty of this farmhouse with the trout stream running past. Let us hope that its owners appreciated what they had and what modern man is now searching for - peace, serenity and calm, far removed from today's madding crowd.

LLANDEILO, Rhosmaen Street 1936 87715
Situated on a high bluff in the heart of the Towy valley, the historic little market town of Llandeilo has many
attractions to offer. Charming from a distance, it does not disappoint on close acquaintance, as this picture of
Rhosmaen Street shows. The narrow and well-kept street is cobwebbed with bunting and flags commemorating
George VI, who was proclaimed King on 12 December 1936.

LLANDEILO
THE BLACK MOUNTAINS 1936 87719A
From the lush and fertile meadow and woodlands, the
Black Mountains form a dramatic backdrop to the
picture. This is the name given to two ranges of hills in
the Brecon Beacons National Park. The two peaks in the
range are Waun Fach, at 2660 feet, and Carmarthen Van,
at 2632 feet, surrounded by two lonely lakes - a left-over
from the Ice Age.

LLANDEILO
DYNEVOR CASTLE c1960 L70053
This is one of the many Welsh place names with two spellings -
the alternative is 'Dinefwr'. Whichever you choose, the castle
has been the seat of Lord Dynevor since his family acquired the
seat in the 9th century. Today, a picturesque 18th-century
landscaped park surrounds Newton House, which was built in
the 17th century but now has a Victorian Gothic façade.

LLANDEILO, CARREG CENNEN CASTLE c1960 L70065
The second castle is Carreg Cennen, a striking fortress south-east of Llandeilo. It has been described as 'a castle like a rock upon a rock', so perfectly do the walls blend with the crags upon which they stand. There is evidence of human activity on the hill as far back as pre-historic times, and there was probably a castle on the site for many years before the existing one was begun at the end of the 13th century.

LLANARTHNEY, THE VILLAGE 1937 87878

This small village is in one of the most fertile parts of the valley of the Towy. At the crest of the hill is a spacious inn called the Golden Grove Arms, directly opposite the church. The contraption on the extreme right of the photograph is a device for bending metal into strips - possibly it was being used here in the construction of barrels.

LLANARTHNEY, THE VILLAGE 1938 88252

This picture was taken looking back down the road. Here there is a better view of the church, which is dedicated to St Teilo, from which the town derives its name. The church was rebuilt in 1848 in the Decorated style, but the tower is Perpendicular. Immediately on the right is an early post office, next to the Emlyn Arms, a rather small hostelry.

LLANDOVERY, THE CASTLE c1960 L258005

Llandovery does not fail to disappoint, with its ruins of just a small fragment of the castle situated on a grassy knoll. It is said to have been erected by the Normans about the year 1100; it was almost immediately seized by the Welsh, who retained possession until the time of Edward I. It is interesting that they put aside their inclination for burning castles down on this occasion.

LLANDOVERY, THE YSTRADFFIN VALLEY c1960 L258046
This, one of the more interesting photos in our tour, again shows the glaciated valley and the circuitous winding road clinging to the hillside. The pristine Austin Healey sports car and its driver seem posed by the Frith photographer, and one could ponder whether this prestigious car did indeed belong to the Friths!

LLANDOVERY, MAESEDDYGON, RHANDIRMWYN C1960 L258018

Taken upstream, this picture shows the fast flowing and rocky nature of the waters. For those of geological bent, this is also a perfect example of a glaciated valley with a well-preserved drumlin, or mound of clay left by the glacier, at the bend in the stream.

LLANDOVERY, DOLAUHURIAN BRIDGE 1962 L258020

The road through the Ystradffin Valley passes under the railway before reaching one of the two bridges at Dolauhurian. One of them carries the road heading towards Cilycwm. Both appear picturesque and ivy-clad, but they are purely functional and not ornate in any way.

LLANDOVERY, GENERAL VIEW C1960 L258023

'A small but beautiful town', was George Borrow's brief description of Llandovery, the trading and market centre for a large agricultural district. The word 'Llandovery' is a corruption of the Welsh Llan-ym-ddyfri, meaning 'the church among the waters'. This is an appropriate name, as the town is situated between the river Towy and many other feeder streams.

LLANDOVERY, THE COLLEGE C1960 L258029

The town also has one of the two Welsh recognised public schools. Llandovery College was a 19th-century foundation; besides having a good academic record, it has also produced some of the finest rugby players in Wales.

LLANDOVERY, THE SUGAR LOAF c1960 L258073

The north-east road out of Llandovery follows the same course as the railway into central Wales. The railway tunnels under the pointed hill known from its appearance as the Sugar Loaf - another awesome glacial feature. In fact, whatever road you take out of Llandovery you find yourself in delectable country.

HALFWAY, THE RIVER AT GUTTO MILL c1955 H492005

The beauty of this village is well worth searching for. Halfway is the tiniest hamlet imaginable, and takes its name from the fact that it is halfway between Lampeter and Llandeilo on the river Gwidderig, which flows south from the Teifi to the Towy.

HALFWAY
Gutto Mill c1955

Unlike the Towy, the river Gwidderig was much faster-flowing, and powered many small mills along its way. Before the advent of steam, in the days when materials and labour came cheap, it was the custom to build a small textile mill wherever there was a good supply of water. This can be seen in many other areas of the British Isles, including the Yorkshire Dales.

HALFWAY
The Village c1955

The steep-sided valleys around the river Gwidderig are lush with woodland; in this scene they gave the photographer a high vantage point from which to look down on the village. The largest house in the centre would appear to be a pub or hotel, very convenient for the post office and general store immediately next door.

HALFWAY, GUTTO MILL c1955 H492001

HALFWAY, THE VILLAGE c1955 H492004

HALFWAY, THE RIVER GWYDDERIG c1955 H492002
As we look upstream here, we can see that the Gwydderig has become so narrow that it barely deserves the title of river. Most of the picture is taken up with the mass of woodland leading down to the riverbank.

HALFWAY, THE HOME OF WILLIAM WILLIAMS (PANT-Y-CELYN) c1955 H492006
This imposing and porched house was once the home of William Williams, one of the three great leaders of the Methodist revival in Wales. Williams was a hymn writer first and foremost; one of his best-known hymns was 'Guide Me O Thou Great Jehovah'. He was also a theologian, a counsellor, a preacher, an instructor and a prodigious writer.

HALFWAY, THE VILLAGE c1955 H492010
We are back down again in the valley bottom. Here, there is a clearer view of the hotel, and at this date a filling station has arrived. The villagers of Halfway were so remote from 'civilisation' that they certainly made their automobiles endure - the solitary car pre-dates the picture by some twenty years.

TALLEY, THE LAKES AND THE ABBEY 1936 87713

This is a genuine beauty spot, with its ruined abbey, two small lakes and green hills all around. The abbey was founded by the Lord Rhys; the monks belonged to the Premonstratensians, who also undertook parish duties. Talley was the only abbey of this order in Wales; it shared the fate of all Welsh monastic institutions when it was razed and pillaged during the Reformation.

TALLEY, THE LAKE 1936 87714

Once the abbey at Talley had gone, there was little left except for the two fresh water lakes. Unfortunately, they are at such a height and so far off the beaten track that they have never been developed for recreation such as boating or swimming.

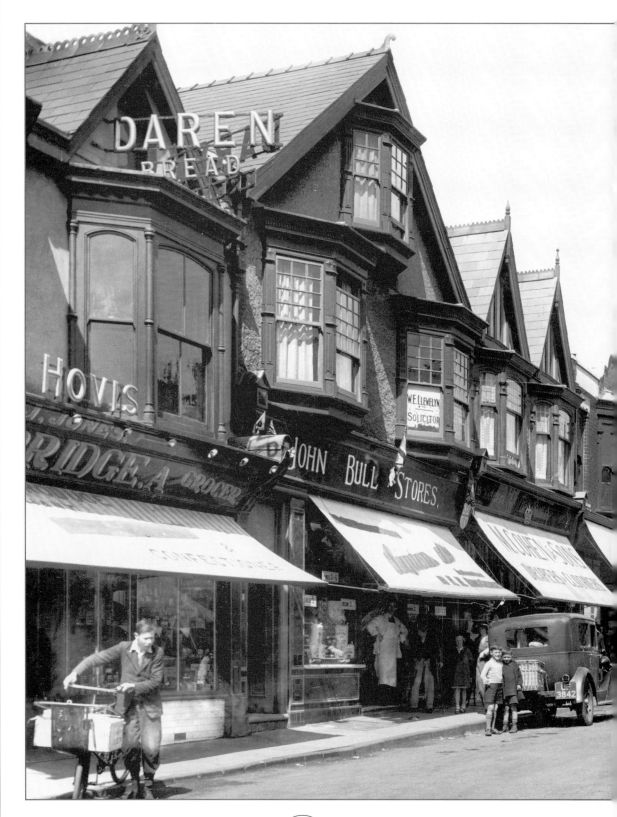

AMMANFORD, QUAY STREET 1936 87811
The steep roofs and gables in the Dutch style overlook a hive of activity in this street scene. The mass of Union Jacks indicates another Royal celebration: this was for the accession of George VI, who was crowned in 1937. In the days before TV advertising, every shop blind played its part in announcing the shop proprietor and his speciality. 'Service with a smile' is evident as the delivery boy sets off on his delivery bike from the premises of Mr Bridge.

AMMANFORD, ALL SAINTS' CHURCH 1936 87809
The church seen here was one of the first parish churches to be newly-built when the town gained its parish status in the 1920s. Originally it was Croffing Church, from the earlier name for Ammanford, and it was built in a neo-Norman style. It is regrettable that the burghers of the town ran out of money and the tower was not finished for many years.

AMMANFORD, THE COUNTY SCHOOL 1936 87810
The builder of the church was employed to work on the County School, and this time he was paid on time. The school is directly opposite the church, and is now known as Amman Valley Comprehensive. Its academic record is good, but its sporting prowess is second to none. It has produced international status players in soccer and in both rugby union and league.

AMMANFORD, THE BOWLING GREEN 1936 87812
In contrast to all the hustle and bustle seen in the main street in photograph No 87811, some gentle recreation for the elders was a pleasant break. The game looks tight here, and the player in the centre awaits the last bowl - an earlier one is very close to the jack. Around the green are some most pleasant houses, which must have been modern ones at the time.

AMMANFORD
GORSEDD HILL 1936 87813
The Gorsedd is synonymous with the Eisteddfod; the latter means 'a sitting of learned men' - thus the Gorsedd is simply an assembly. Wherever an assembly was held (and the one here was in 1922) a stone circle was traditionally erected. In the picture it makes a useful place for relaxation, but originally it was a pagan ceremony, and the stone circle no doubt had a more quasi-religious function.

AMMANFORD, COLLEGE STREET c1955 A186019

The streets of Ammanford were certainly very busy places, even if the roads were not very well kept. Virtually everything that the locals required can be seen here. On the left it is only a few steps from the Midland Bank to the Palace Cinema, and directly across the road quite a crowd have gathered outside the Star Supply Stores. Next door is Gabes' Booksellers, from where it is not far to a quiet pint at either the Cross or the Old Cross Inn.

AMMANFORD, TIRYDAIL LANE AND BETTWS MOUNTAIN c1955 A186027

The roundabout at the junction of these two roads is certainly well-kept by the parks department. It is good that this is a wet area, as the hanging baskets would be difficult to water! With the apparent total absence of traffic, it seems optimistic to tell it to keep left. This would be a better-class area of Ammanford: everything is in perfect order, including the roadway, the pavements, the hedges and the houses.

GARNANT, GLYN-HIR FALLS 1936 87761

As the tour of Carmarthenshire comes almost to its end, no tour would be complete without a waterfall. The words serenity, tranquillity and natural beauty tumble out as fast as the Glyn-Hir Falls.

GARNANT, THE BETHEL CHAPEL 1936 87760

The Methodists and their associated non-conformist religions were never ones for ornate decoration. The chapels were purely functional, so as to focus minds on their true purpose. This cannot be better exemplified than at the Bethel Chapel shown here.

BRYNAMMON, THE PUBLIC HALL c1940 B471003

The Public Hall here is something of a misnomer, as at this time it is being used as a cinema. The lucky people had a choice of two films: 'Sergeant Murphy' and 'The Amazing Doctor Clitterhouse', the former starring Ronald Reagan and the latter with Edward G Robinson and Humphrey Bogart.

BRYNAMMAN, THE SWIMMING POOL c1955 B471006

The youngsters of the area are lucky to have such a mild climate; the open-air swimming pool can be used almost all year round. This is no leisure pool, for the three boys on the pool side are awaiting their instructions. In the event of any child getting into difficulty, the heavy clothing of the teacher in attendance would not be much use for life saving.

BRYNAMMAN, THE WELSH SCHOOL c1955 B471005

Of all the wonderful sights, both natural and man made, that we have seen in Carmarthenshire, the schoolhouse here has little to commend it. It is purely functional, and judging by the size of the windows, not much thought went into light and airy classrooms. The total absence of any children does not necessarily indicate a holiday, as they could be slaving away at their desks.

BRYNAMMAN, GENERAL VIEW c1955 B471007

This is a more distant shot of the swimming pool, taken from a higher vantage point. It is an unfortunate coincidence that immediately to the left of the pool is a graveyard. The railway crosses the picture from left to right, and the houses appear to be built on three levels. The first is on the roadside, the second is above the railway and the third is even higher up the valley.

BRYNAMMAN, THE POST OFFICE c1955 B471009
The Post Office and the adjoining telephone box nestle conveniently at the junction of three roads, which is also a gathering point for local gossip. The advertising sign on the gable end of the Post Office is for Wills 'Flag' cigarettes.

BRYNAMMAN, THE VILLAGE c1955 B471011
This view looks north-west from above; the village is spread out below, and once more there is a virtually empty road. The largest building in view is a purely functional place of worship, the Ebenezer Independent Chapel, which was erected at the turn of the century. It also serves the purpose of being the exact boundary between Swansea and Carmarthenshire.

BRYNAMMAN, THE PARISH CHURCH c1955 B471020
This photograph shows St Catherine's church, which was originally constructed in 1891. It is unfortunate that during World War II a bomber missed its target of Swansea by a considerable distance and the church roof was badly damaged. It was eventually repaired in 1945.

BRYNAMMAN, THE WATERFALL c1955 B471012
In the spiritual world, water symbolises the emotions, and an image such as this would arouse feelings of calm. The youngsters of the area would, no doubt, take delight in swimming in the rock pool and investigating the myriad aquatic life in the cool waters.

PENSARN, WELSH COSTUMES 1895 36593
The tall hat, frilled mob-cap, and shawl seen here were still worn by Carmarthen women at the turn of the century.
Today they are only likely to be seen in the summer season for the benefit and amusement of tourists.

Index

Frith Book Co Titles

www.francisfrith.co.uk

The Frith Book Company publishes over 100 new titles each year. A selection of those currently available are listed below. For latest catalogue please contact Frith Book Co.

Town Books 96 pages, approx 100 photos. County and Themed Books 128 pages, approx 150 photos (unless specified). All titles hardback laminated case and jacket except those indicated pb (paperback)

Amersham, Chesham & Rickmansworth (pb)			Derby (pb)	1-85937-367-4	£9.99
	1-85937-340-2	£9.99	Derbyshire (pb)	1-85937-196-5	£9.99
Ancient Monuments & Stone Circles	1-85937-143-4	£17.99	Devon (pb)	1-85937-297-x	£9.99
Aylesbury (pb)	1-85937-227-9	£9.99	Dorset (pb)	1-85937-269-4	£9.99
Bakewell	1-85937-113-2	£12.99	Dorset Churches	1-85937-172-8	£17.99
Barnstaple (pb)	1-85937-300-3	£9.99	Dorset Coast (pb)	1-85937-299-6	£9.99
Bath (pb)	1-85937419-0	£9.99	Dorset Living Memories	1-85937-210-4	£14.99
Bedford (pb)	1-85937-205-8	£9.99	Down the Severn	1-85937-118-3	£14.99
Berkshire (pb)	1-85937-191-4	£9.99	Down the Thames (pb)	1-85937-278-3	£9.99
Berkshire Churches	1-85937-170-1	£17.99	Down the Trent	1-85937-311-9	£14.99
Blackpool (pb)	1-85937-382-8	£9.99	Dublin (pb)	1-85937-231-7	£9.99
Bognor Regis (pb)	1-85937-431-x	£9.99	East Anglia (pb)	1-85937-265-1	£9.99
Bournemouth	1-85937-067-5	£12.99	East London	1-85937-080-2	£14.99
Bradford (pb)	1-85937-204-x	£9.99	East Sussex	1-85937-130-2	£14.99
Brighton & Hove(pb)	1-85937-192-2	£8.99	Eastbourne	1-85937-061-6	£12.99
Bristol (pb)	1-85937-264-3	£9.99	Edinburgh (pb)	1-85937-193-0	£8.99
British Life A Century Ago (pb)	1-85937-213-9	£9.99	England in the 1880s	1-85937-331-3	£17.99
Buckinghamshire (pb)	1-85937-200-7	£9.99	English Castles (pb)	1-85937-434-4	£9.99
Camberley (pb)	1-85937-222-8	£9.99	English Country Houses	1-85937-161-2	£17.99
Cambridge (pb)	1-85937-422-0	£9.99	Essex (pb)	1-85937-270-8	£9.99
Cambridgeshire (pb)	1-85937-420-4	£9.99	Exeter	1-85937-126-4	£12.99
Canals & Waterways (pb)	1-85937-291-0	£9.99	Exmoor	1-85937-132-9	£14.99
Canterbury Cathedral (pb)	1-85937-179-5	£9.99	Falmouth	1-85937-066-7	£12.99
Cardiff (pb)	1-85937-093-4	£9.99	Folkestone (pb)	1-85937-124-8	£9.99
Carmarthenshire	1-85937-216-3	£14.99	Glasgow (pb)	1-85937-190-6	£9.99
Chelmsford (pb)	1-85937-310-0	£9.99	Gloucestershire	1-85937-102-7	£14.99
Cheltenham (pb)	1-85937-095-0	£9.99	Great Yarmouth (pb)	1-85937-426-3	£9.99
Cheshire (pb)	1-85937-271-6	£9.99	Greater Manchester (pb)	1-85937-266-x	£9.99
Chester	1-85937-090-x	£12.99	Guildford (pb)	1-85937-410-7	£9.99
Chesterfield	1-85937-378-x	£9.99	Hampshire (pb)	1-85937-279-1	£9.99
Chichester (pb)	1-85937-228-7	£9.99	Hampshire Churches (pb)	1-85937-207-4	£9.99
Colchester (pb)	1-85937-188-4	£8.99	Harrogate	1-85937-423-9	£9.99
Cornish Coast	1-85937-163-9	£14.99	Hastings & Bexhill (pb)	1-85937-131-0	£9.99
Cornwall (pb)	1-85937-229-5	£9.99	Heart of Lancashire (pb)	1-85937-197-3	£9.99
Cornwall Living Memories	1-85937-248-1	£14.99	Helston (pb)	1-85937-214-7	£9.99
Cotswolds (pb)	1-85937-230-9	£9.99	Hereford (pb)	1-85937-175-2	£9.99
Cotswolds Living Memories	1-85937-255-4	£14.99	Herefordshire	1-85937-174-4	£14.99
County Durham	1-85937-123-x	£14.99	Hertfordshire (pb)	1-85937-247-3	£9.99
Croydon Living Memories	1-85937-162-0	£9.99	Horsham (pb)	1-85937-432-8	£9.99
Cumbria	1-85937-101-9	£14.99	Humberside	1-85937-215-5	£14.99
Dartmoor	1-85937-145-0	£14.99	Hythe, Romney Marsh & Ashford	1-85937-256-2	£9.99

Available from your local bookshop or from the publisher

Frith Book Co Titles (continued)

Title	ISBN	Price	Title	ISBN	Price
Ipswich (pb)	1-85937-424-7	£9.99	St Ives (pb)	1-85937415-8	£9.99
Ireland (pb)	1-85937-181-7	£9.99	Scotland (pb)	1-85937-182-5	£9.99
Isle of Man (pb)	1-85937-268-6	£9.99	Scottish Castles (pb)	1-85937-323-2	£9.99
Isles of Scilly	1-85937-136-1	£14.99	Sevenoaks & Tunbridge	1-85937-057-8	£12.99
Isle of Wight (pb)	1-85937-429-8	£9.99	Sheffield, South Yorks (pb)	1-85937-267-8	£9.99
Isle of Wight Living Memories	1-85937-304-6	£14.99	Shrewsbury (pb)	1-85937-325-9	£9.99
Kent (pb)	1-85937-189-2	£9.99	Shropshire (pb)	1-85937-326-7	£9.99
Kent Living Memories	1-85937-125-6	£14.99	Somerset	1-85937-153-1	£14.99
Lake District (pb)	1-85937-275-9	£9.99	South Devon Coast	1-85937-107-8	£14.99
Lancaster, Morecambe & Heysham (pb)	1-85937-233-3	£9.99	South Devon Living Memories	1-85937-168-x	£14.99
Leeds (pb)	1-85937-202-3	£9.99	South Hams	1-85937-220-1	£14.99
Leicester	1-85937-073-x	£12.99	Southampton (pb)	1-85937-427-1	£9.99
Leicestershire (pb)	1-85937-185-x	£9.99	Southport (pb)	1-85937-425-5	£9.99
Lincolnshire (pb)	1-85937-433-6	£9.99	Staffordshire	1-85937-047-0	£12.99
Liverpool & Merseyside (pb)	1-85937-234-1	£9.99	Stratford upon Avon	1-85937-098-5	£12.99
London (pb)	1-85937-183-3	£9.99	Suffolk (pb)	1-85937-221-x	£9.99
Ludlow (pb)	1-85937-176-0	£9.99	Suffolk Coast	1-85937-259-7	£14.99
Luton (pb)	1-85937-235-x	£9.99	Surrey (pb)	1-85937-240-6	£9.99
Maidstone	1-85937-056-x	£14.99	Sussex (pb)	1-85937-184-1	£9.99
Manchester (pb)	1-85937-198-1	£9.99	Swansea (pb)	1-85937-167-1	£9.99
Middlesex	1-85937-158-2	£14.99	Tees Valley & Cleveland	1-85937-211-2	£14.99
New Forest	1-85937-128-0	£14.99	Thanet (pb)	1-85937-116-7	£9.99
Newark (pb)	1-85937-366-6	£9.99	Tiverton (pb)	1-85937-178-7	£9.99
Newport, Wales (pb)	1-85937-258-9	£9.99	Torbay	1-85937-063-2	£12.99
Newquay (pb)	1-85937-421-2	£9.99	Truro	1-85937-147-7	£12.99
Norfolk (pb)	1-85937-195-7	£9.99	Victorian and Edwardian Cornwall	1-85937-252-x	£14.99
Norfolk Living Memories	1-85937-217-1	£14.99	Victorian & Edwardian Devon	1-85937-253-8	£14.99
Northamptonshire	1-85937-150-7	£14.99	Victorian & Edwardian Kent	1-85937-149-3	£14.99
Northumberland Tyne & Wear (pb)	1-85937-281-3	£9.99	Vic & Ed Maritime Album	1-85937-144-2	£17.99
North Devon Coast	1-85937-146-9	£14.99	Victorian and Edwardian Sussex	1-85937-157-4	£14.99
North Devon Living Memories	1-85937-261-9	£14.99	Victorian & Edwardian Yorkshire	1-85937-154-x	£14.99
North London	1-85937-206-6	£14.99	Victorian Seaside	1-85937-159-0	£17.99
North Wales (pb)	1-85937-298-8	£9.99	Villages of Devon (pb)	1-85937-293-7	£9.99
North Yorkshire (pb)	1-85937-236-8	£9.99	Villages of Kent (pb)	1-85937-294-5	£9.99
Norwich (pb)	1-85937-194-9	£8.99	Villages of Sussex (pb)	1-85937-295-3	£9.99
Nottingham (pb)	1-85937-324-0	£9.99	Warwickshire (pb)	1-85937-203-1	£9.99
Nottinghamshire (pb)	1-85937-187-6	£9.99	Welsh Castles (pb)	1-85937-322-4	£9.99
Oxford (pb)	1-85937-411-5	£9.99	West Midlands (pb)	1-85937-289-9	£9.99
Oxfordshire (pb)	1-85937-430-1	£9.99	West Sussex	1-85937-148-5	£14.99
Peak District (pb)	1-85937-280-5	£9.99	West Yorkshire (pb)	1-85937-201-5	£9.99
Penzance	1-85937-069-1	£12.99	Weymouth (pb)	1-85937-209-0	£9.99
Peterborough (pb)	1-85937-219-8	£9.99	Wiltshire (pb)	1-85937-277-5	£9.99
Piers	1-85937-237-6	£17.99	Wiltshire Churches (pb)	1-85937-171-x	£9.99
Plymouth	1-85937-119-1	£12.99	Wiltshire Living Memories	1-85937-245-7	£14.99
Poole & Sandbanks (pb)	1-85937-251-1	£9.99	Winchester (pb)	1-85937-428-x	£9.99
Preston (pb)	1-85937-212-0	£9.99	Windmills & Watermills	1-85937-242-2	£17.99
Reading (pb)	1-85937-238-4	£9.99	Worcester (pb)	1-85937-165-5	£9.99
Romford (pb)	1-85937-319-4	£9.99	Worcestershire	1-85937-152-3	£14.99
Salisbury (pb)	1-85937-239-2	£9.99	York (pb)	1-85937-199-x	£9.99
Scarborough (pb)	1-85937-379-8	£9.99	Yorkshire (pb)	1-85937-186-8	£9.99
St Albans (pb)	1-85937-341-0	£9.99	Yorkshire Living Memories	1-85937-166-3	£14.99

See Frith books on the internet www.francisfrith.co.uk

FRITH PRODUCTS & SERVICES

Francis Frith would doubtless be pleased to know that the pioneering publishing venture he started in 1860 still continues today. A hundred and forty years later, The Francis Frith Collection continues in the same innovative tradition and is now one of the foremost publishers of vintage photographs in the world. Some of the current activities include:

Interior Decoration

Today Frith's photographs can be seen framed and as giant wall murals in thousands of pubs, restaurants, hotels, banks, retail stores and other public buildings throughout the country. In every case they enhance the unique local atmosphere of the places they depict and provide reminders of gentler days in an increasingly busy and frenetic world.

Product Promotions

Frith products are used by many major companies to promote the sales of their own products or to reinforce their own history and heritage. Frith promotions have been used by Hovis bread, Courage beers, Scots Porage Oats, Colman's mustard, Cadbury's foods, Mellow Birds coffee, Dunhill pipe tobacco, Guinness, and Bulmer's Cider.

Genealogy and Family History

As the interest in family history and roots grows world-wide, more and more people are turning to Frith's photographs of Great Britain for images of the towns, villages and streets where their ancestors lived; and, of course, photographs of the churches and chapels where their ancestors were christened, married and buried are an essential part of every genealogy tree and family album.

Frith Products

All Frith photographs are available Framed or just as Mounted Prints and Posters (size 23 x 16 inches). These may be ordered from the address below. From time to time other products - Address Books, Calendars, Table Mats, etc - are available.

The Internet

Already twenty thousand Frith photographs can be viewed and purchased on the internet through the Frith websites and a myriad of partner sites.

For more detailed information on Frith companies and products, look at these sites:

www.francisfrith.co.uk
www.francisfrith.com
(for North American visitors)

See the complete list of Frith Books at:

www.francisfrith.co.uk

This web site is regularly updated with the latest list of publications from the Frith Book Company. If you wish to buy books relating to another part of the country that your local bookshop does not stock, you may purchase on-line.

For further information, trade, or author enquiries please contact us at the address below:
The Francis Frith Collection, Frith's Barn, Teffont, Salisbury, Wiltshire, England SP3 5QP.
Tel: +44 (0)1722 716 376 Fax: +44 (0)1722 716 881 Email: sales@francisfrith.co.uk

---

See Frith books on the internet www.francisfrith.co.uk

TO RECEIVE YOUR **FREE** MOUNTED PRINT

Mounted Print
Overall size 14 x 11 inches

Cut out this Voucher and return it with your remittance for £1.95 to cover postage and handling, to UK addresses. For overseas addresses please include £4.00 post and handling. Choose any photograph included in this book. Your SEPIA print will be A4 in size, and mounted in a cream mount with burgundy rule line, overall size 14 x 11 inches.

Order additional Mounted Prints at HALF PRICE (only £7.49 each*)

If there are further pictures you would like to order, possibly as gifts for friends and family, purchase them at half price (no additional postage and handling required).

Have your Mounted Prints framed*

For an additional £14.95 per print you can have your chosen Mounted Print framed in an elegant polished wood and gilt moulding, overall size 16 x 13 inches (no additional postage and handling required).

---

* IMPORTANT!
These special prices are only available if ordered using the original voucher on this page (no copies permitted) and at the same time as your free Mounted Print, for delivery to the same address

---

Frith Collectors' Guild

From time to time we publish a magazine of news and stories about Frith photographs and further special offers of Frith products. If you would like 12 months FREE membership, please return this form.

Send completed forms to:
The Francis Frith Collection, Frith's Barn, Teffont, Salisbury, Wiltshire SP3 5QP

Voucher for **FREE** and Reduced Price Frith Prints

Picture no.	Page number	Qty	Mounted @ £7.49	Framed + £14.95	Total Cost
		1	**Free of charge***	£	£
			£7.49	£	£
			£7.49	£	£
			£7.49	£	£
			£7.49	£	£
			£7.49	£	£

Please allow 28 days for delivery *** Post & handling**	**£1.95**
Book Title . . . . **Total Order Cost**	**£**

Please do not photocopy this voucher. Only the original is valid, so please cut it out and return it to us.

I enclose a cheque / postal order for £ . . . .
made payable to 'The Francis Frith Collection'
OR please debit my Mastercard / Visa / Switch / Amex card
(credit cards please on all overseas orders)

Number . . . .

Issue No(Switch only) . . . . .Valid from (Amex/Switch) . . . .

Expires . . . . Signature . . . .

Name Mr/Mrs/Ms . . . .

Address . . . .

. . . .

. . . . Postcode . . . .

Daytime Tel No . . . .   Valid to 31/12/03

The Francis Frith Collectors' Guild

Please enrol me as a member for 12 months free of charge.

Name Mr/Mrs/Ms . . . .

Address . . . .

. . . .

. . . . Postcode . . . .

Would you like to find out more about Francis Frith?

We have recently recruited some entertaining speakers who are happy to visit local groups, clubs and societies to give an illustrated talk documenting Frith's travels and photographs. If you are a member of such a group and are interested in hosting a presentation, we would love to hear from you.

Our speakers bring with them a small selection of our local town and county books, together with sample prints. They are happy to take orders. A small proportion of the order value is donated to the group who have hosted the presentation. The talks are therefore an excellent way of fundraising for small groups and societies.

Can you help us with information about any of the Frith photographs in this book?

We are gradually compiling an historical record for each of the photographs in the Frith archive. It is always fascinating to find out the names of the people shown in the pictures, as well as insights into the shops, buildings and other features depicted.

If you recognize anyone in the photographs in this book, or if you have information not already included in the author's caption, do let us know. We would love to hear from you, and will try to publish it in future books or articles.

Our production team

Frith books are produced by a small dedicated team at offices in the converted Grade II listed 18th-century barn at Teffont near Salisbury, illustrated above. Most have worked with the Frith Collection for many years. All have in common one quality: they have a passion for the Frith Collection. The team is constantly expanding, but currently includes:

Jason Buck, John Buck, Douglas Burns, Heather Crisp, Lucy Elcock, Isobel Hall, Rob Hames, Hazel Heaton, Peter Horne, James Kinnear, Tina Leary, Hannah Marsh, Eliza Sackett, Terence Sackett, Sandra Sanger, Lewis Taylor, Shelley Tolcher, Helen Vimpany, Clive Wathen and Jenny Wathen.